THE VERY BEST OF
David Lee Roth

ISBN 0-634-07970-0

HAL•LEONARD®
CORPORATION
7777 W. BLUEMOUND RD. P.O. BOX 13819 MILWAUKEE, WI 53213

Visit Hal Leonard Online at
www.halleonard.com

contents

AIN'T TALKIN' 'BOUT LOVE

Words and Music by DAVID LEE ROTH,
EDWARD VAN HALEN, ALEX VAN HALEN
and MICHAEL ANTHONY

Medium Hard Rock beat

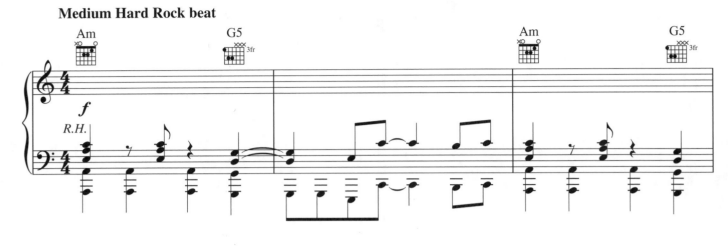

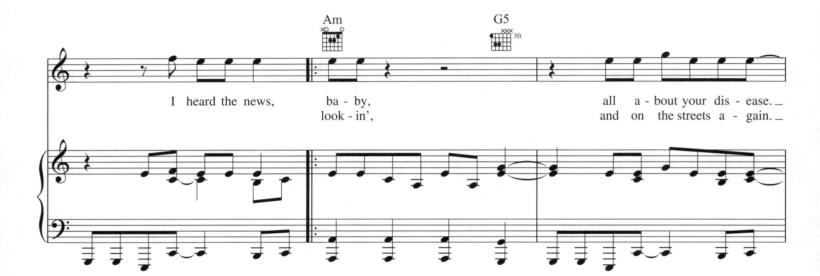

I heard the news,   ba - by,   all   a - bout your dis - ease.___
look - in',   and on   the streets a - gain.___

— Yeah, you   may have all you want,___   ba - by,
— Oh yeah, you think you're real - ly cook - in', ba - by.

and there I stood and looked down.

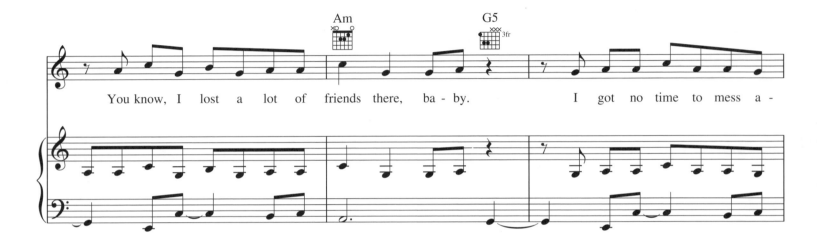

You know, I lost a lot of friends there, ba - by. I got no time to mess a -

round. So if you want it, got to bleed for it, ba - by.

You got to, got to bleed, ba - by. Mm, you got to, got to

bleed, ba - by.   You got to, got to bleed, ba - by.

D.S. al Coda

Ain't talk - in' 'bout

CODA

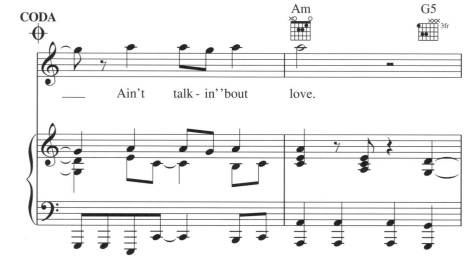

___ Ain't talk - in' 'bout love.

Don't wan - na talk a - bout love.   Don't need to talk a - bout

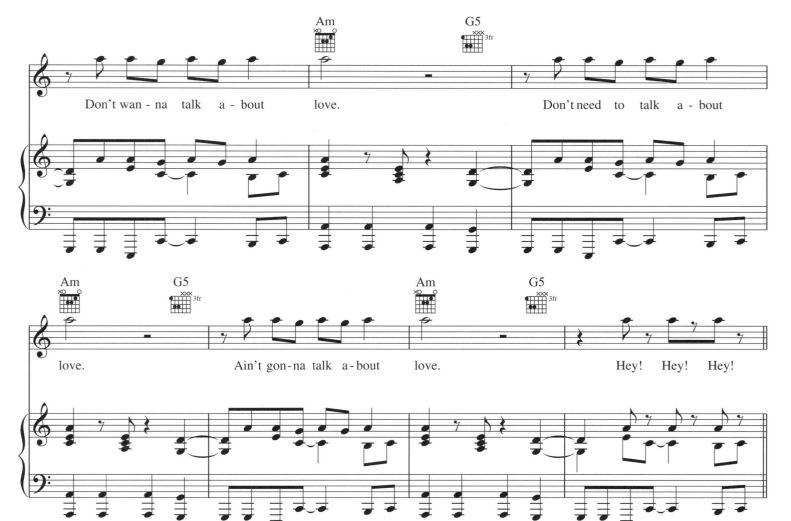

love.   Ain't gon - na talk a - bout love.   Hey! Hey! Hey!

Hey! Hey! Hey!

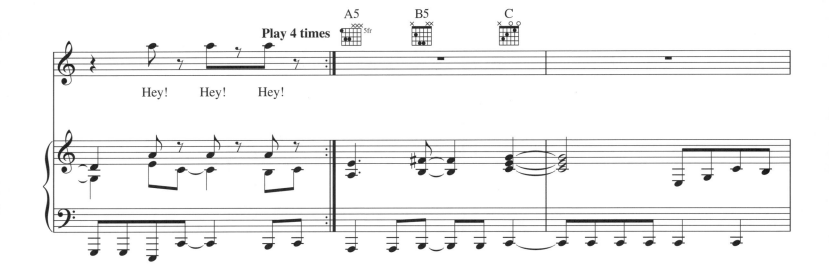

Hey! Hey! Hey!

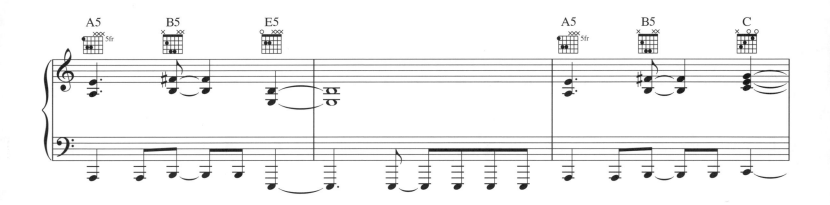

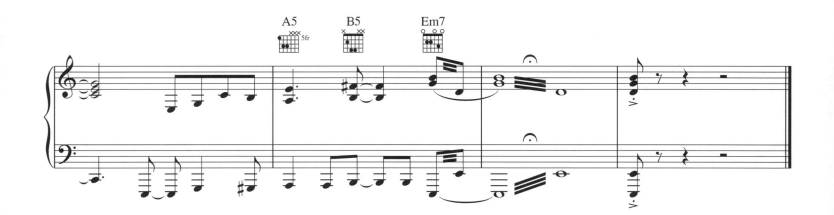

AND THE CRADLE WILL ROCK

Words and Music by DAVID LEE ROTH,
EDWARD VAN HALEN, ALEX VAN HALEN
and MICHAEL ANTHONY

Medium Hard Rock beat

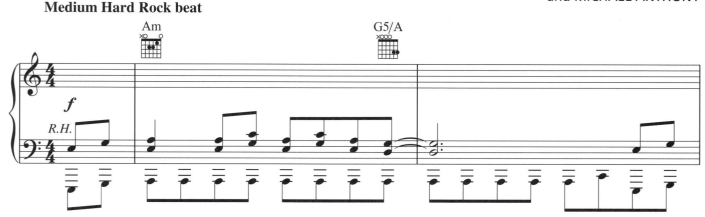

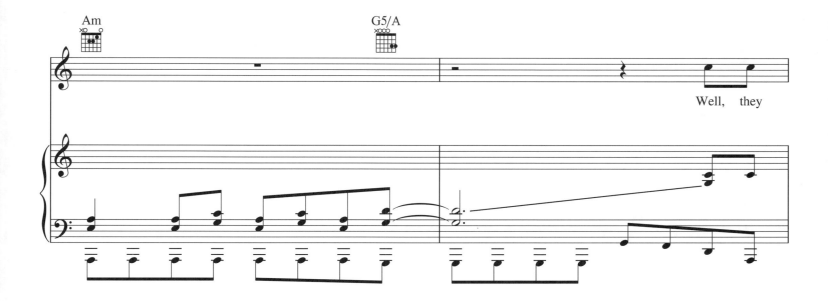

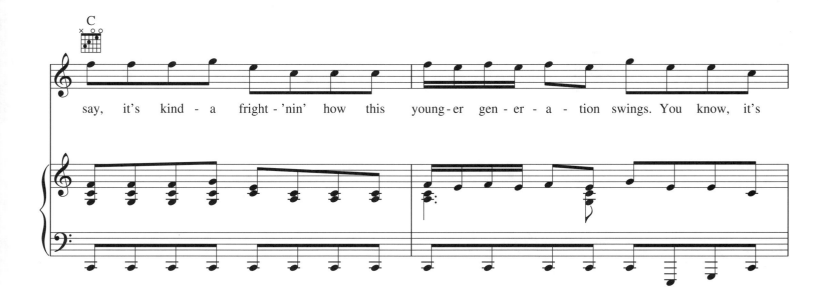

Lyrics: Well, they say, it's kind-a fright-'nin' how this young-er gen-er-a-tion swings. You know, it's

cra - dle will rock. _____ Yeah, the cra - dle will rock. _

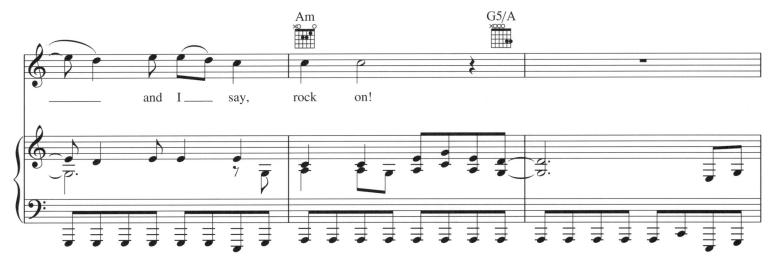

_____ and I ___ say, rock on!

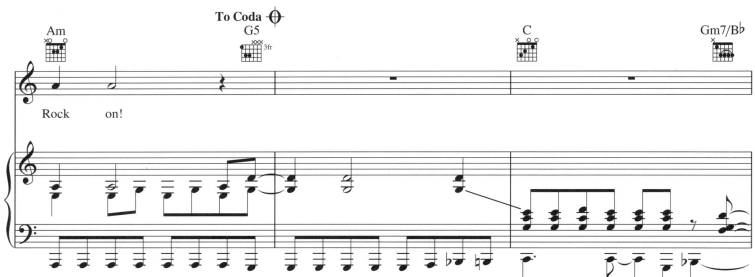

To Coda ⊕

Rock on!

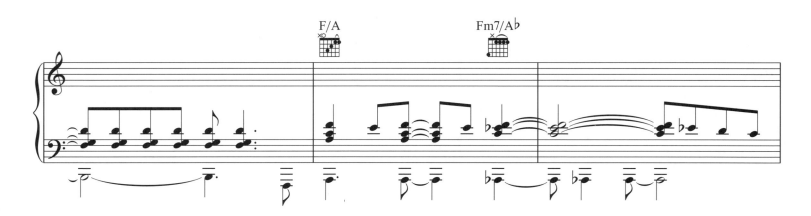

BEAUTIFUL GIRLS

Words and Music by DAVID LEE ROTH,
EDWARD VAN HALEN, ALEX VAN HALEN
and MICHAEL ANTHONY

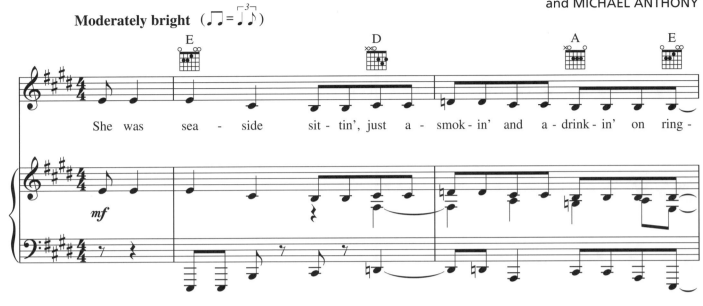

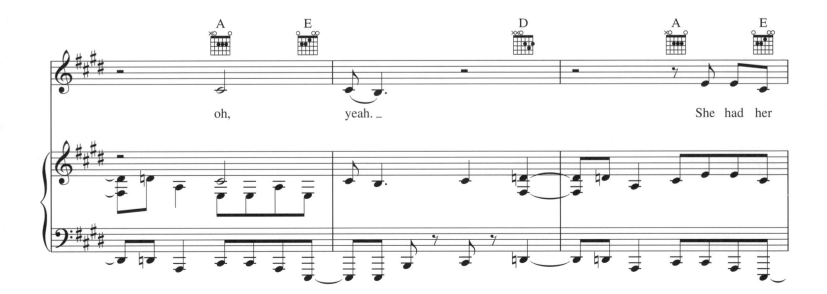

from the sea with the looks to me ___ like she'd like to fool a -

round. What a snap-py lit-tle mam-my. Gon - na keep her pap-py hap - py and ac -

com - pa - ny me ___ to the ends of the earth,

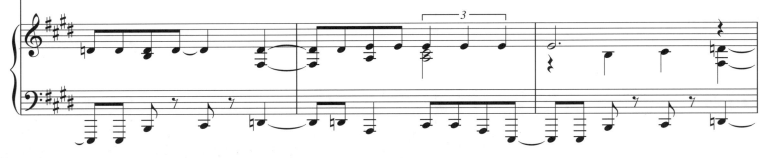

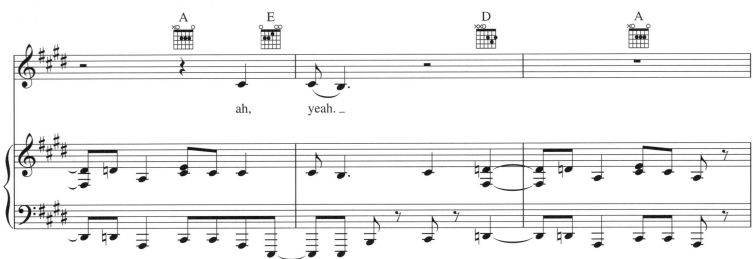

ah, yeah. ___

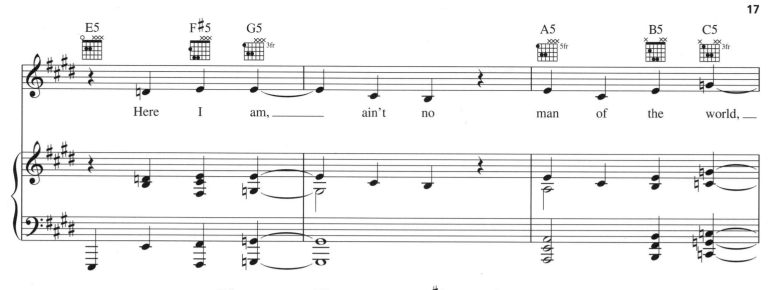

Here I am, _____ ain't no man of the world, _____

_____ no. _____ All I need _____ is a

beau - ti - ful girl. _____ Ah,

yeah! Beau - ti - ful girls.

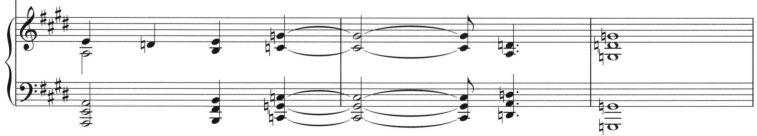

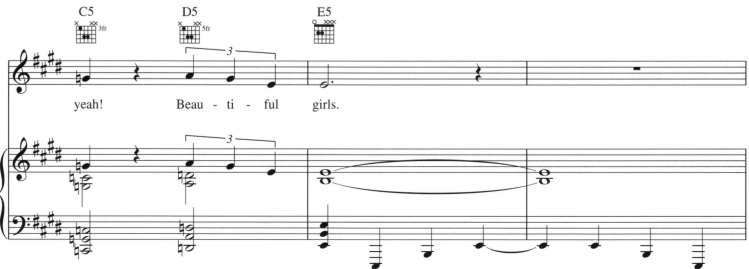

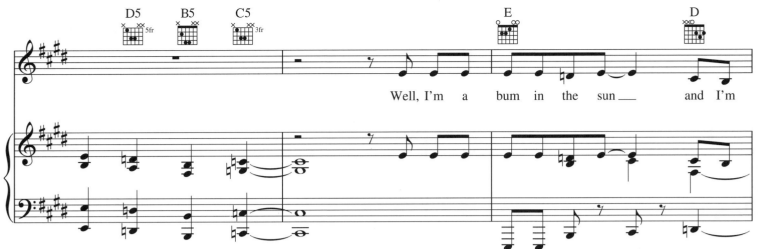

Well, I'm a bum in the sun ___ and I'm

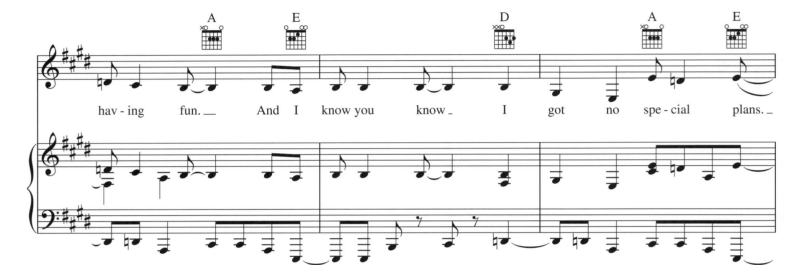

hav-ing fun. ___ And I know you know ___ I got no spe-cial plans. ___

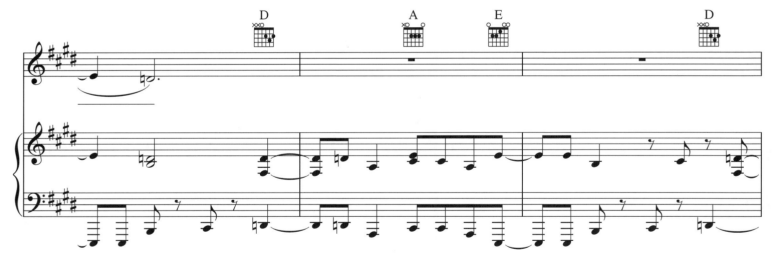

All the bills are paid. ___ I got it made in the shade, and

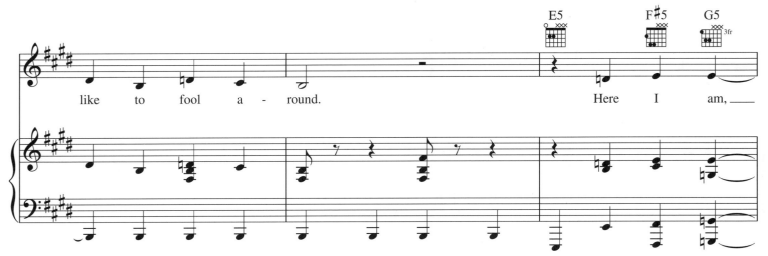

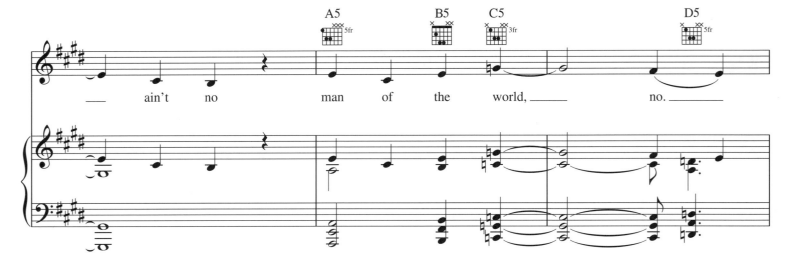

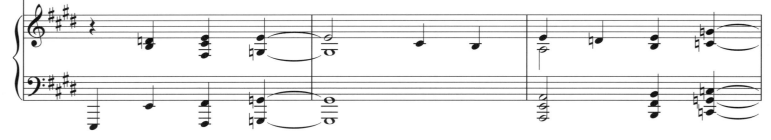

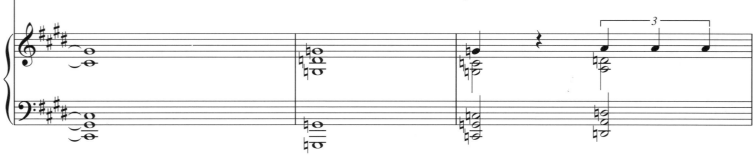

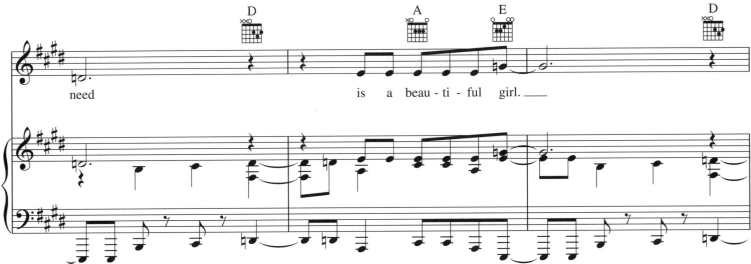

need   is a beau-ti-ful girl. ___

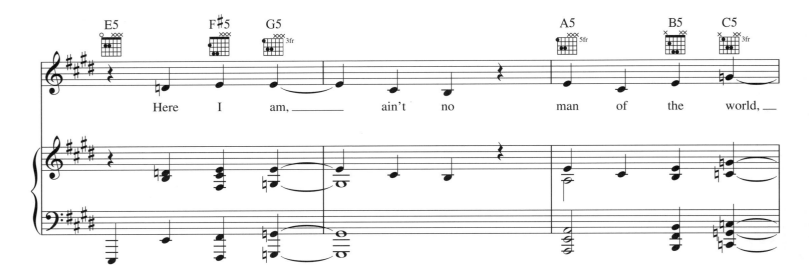

Here I am, ___ ain't no   man   of the world, ___

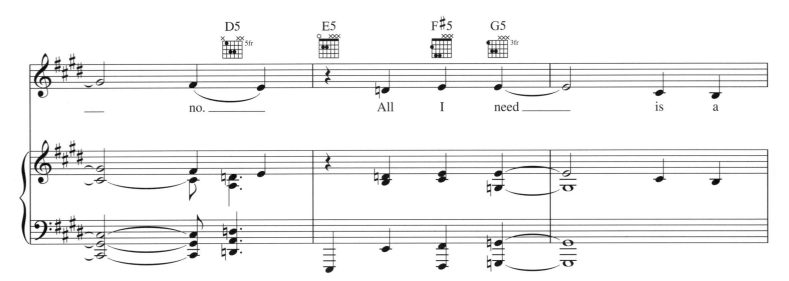

___   no. ___   All I need ___   is a

CALIFORNIA GIRLS

Words and Music by BRIAN WILSON
and MIKE LOVE

Well,

East Coast girls are hip, ___ I real-ly dig ___ those styles they wear; ___
West Coast has the sun-shine, and ___ the girls ___ all get so tanned; ___

Recorded one half step higher.

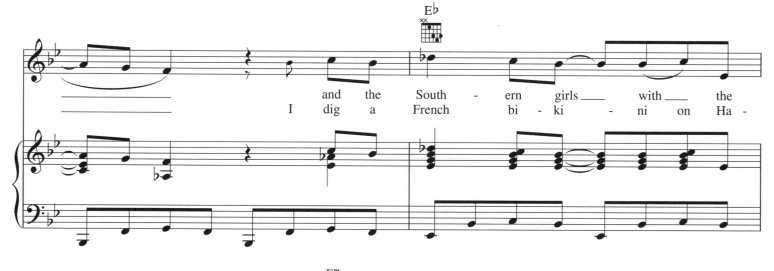

and the South - ern girls ___ with ___ the
I dig a French bi - ki - ni on Ha -

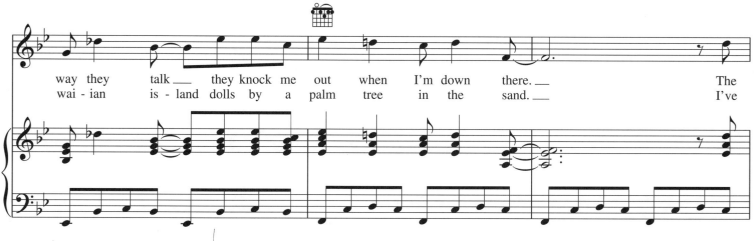

way they talk ___ they knock me out when I'm down there. ___ The
wai - ian is - land dolls by a palm tree in the sand. ___ I've

Mid - west farm - er's daugh - ters real - ly make you feel al - right. ___
been all a - round this great ___ big world, and I've seen all kinds of girls. ___

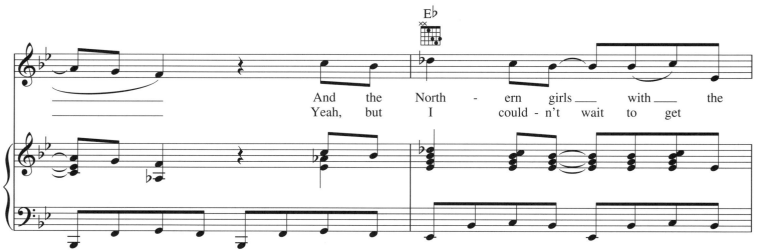

And the North - ern girls ___ with ___ the
Yeah, but I could - n't wait to get

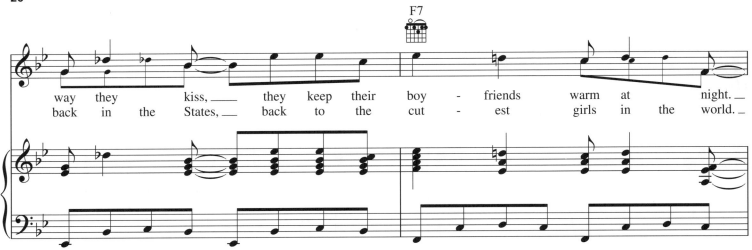

way they kiss, ___ they keep their boy - friends warm at night.
back in the States, ___ back to the cut - est girls in the world. ___

___ } I wish they all could be ___ Cal - i - for - nia, I

wish they all could be ___ Cal - i - for - nia, I wish they all could be ___

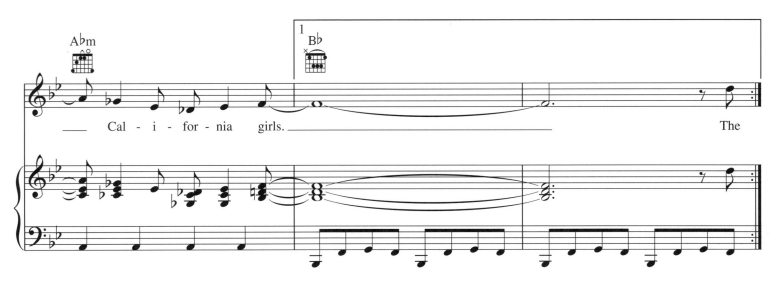

___ Cal - i - for - nia girls. ___ The

I wish they all could be ____ Cal - i - for - nia, I
wish they all could be ____ Cal - i - for - nia, I

Repeat and Fade

Optional Ending

____ Cal - i - for - nia girls. ____

DANCE THE NIGHT AWAY

Words and Music by DAVID LEE ROTH,
EDWARD VAN HALEN, ALEX VAN HALEN
and MICHAEL ANTHONY

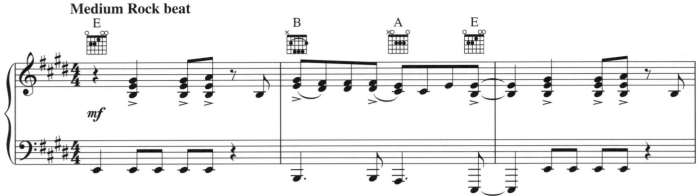

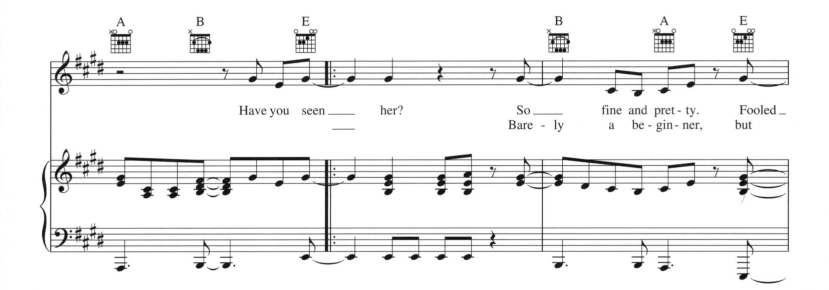

Have you seen ____ her? So ____ fine and pret - ty. Fooled ____
____ Bare - ly a be - gin - ner, but

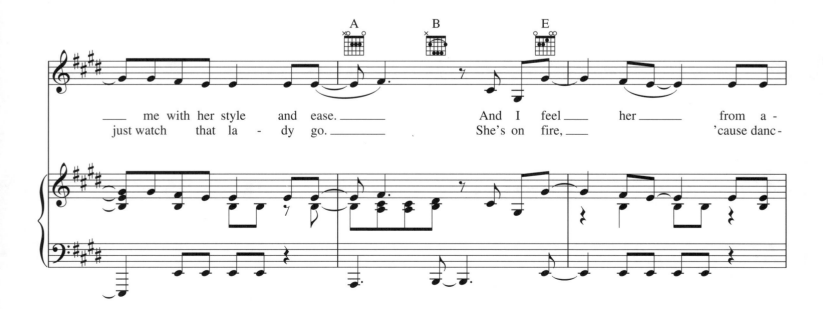

____ me with her style and ease. ____ And I feel ____ her ____ from a -
just watch that la - dy go. ____ She's on fire, ____ 'cause danc -

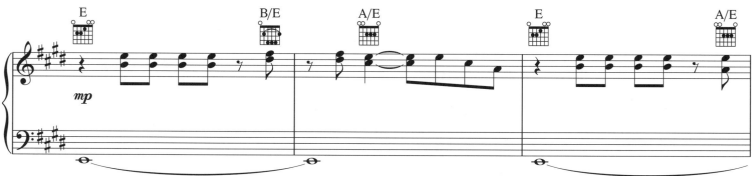

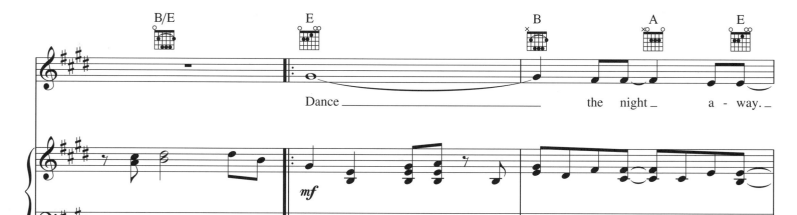

Dance _____ the night _ a - way. _

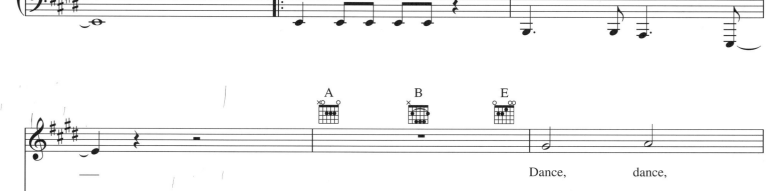

Dance, dance,

Repeat and Fade

dance the night _ a - way. ___

GOIN' CRAZY

Words by DAVID LEE ROTH
Music by STEVE VAI

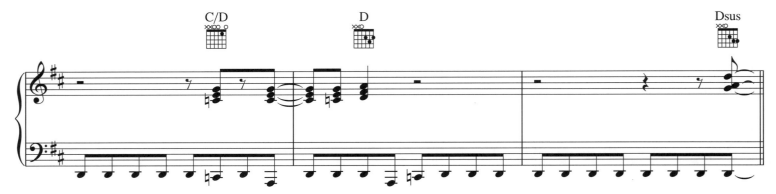

Well, here I'm roll-in' down an-oth-er sun-ny high-way; been in the sun too long.___
Re-mem-ber danc-ing on the pier last night? Got drunk and fell in-to the

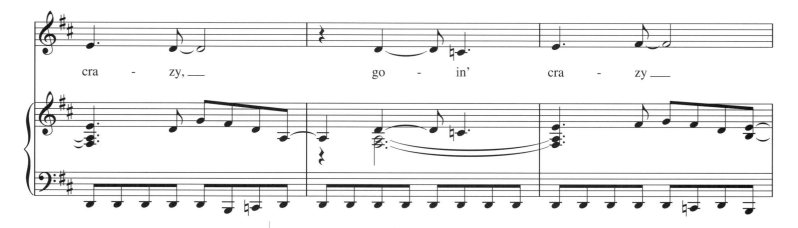

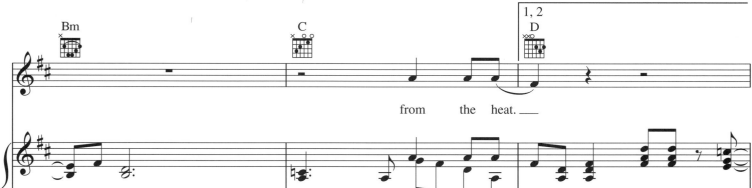

I'LL WAIT

Words and Music by DAVID LEE ROTH,
EDWARD VAN HALEN, ALEX VAN HALEN
and MICHAEL McDONALD

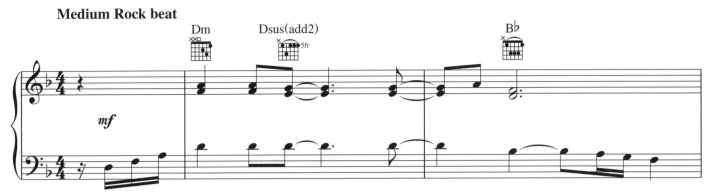

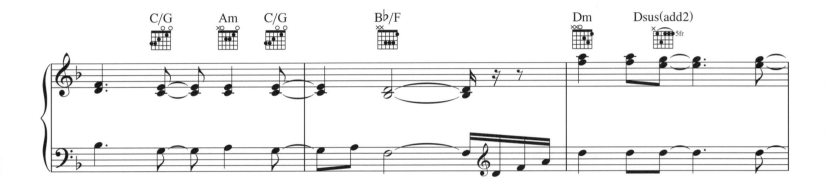

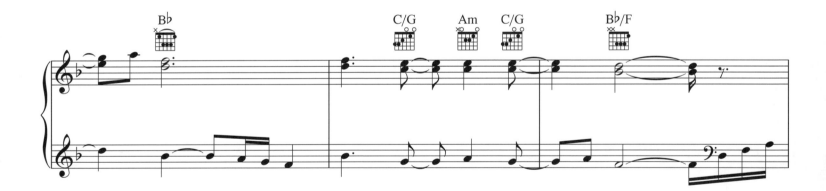

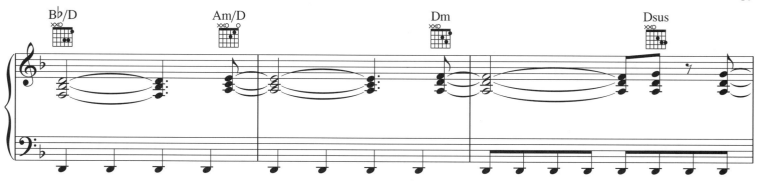

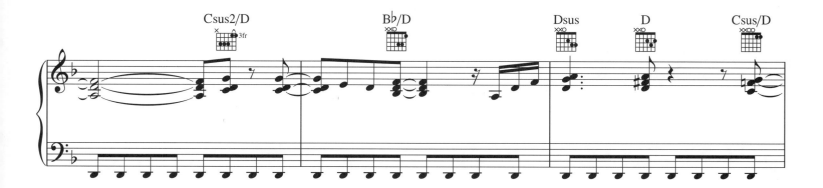

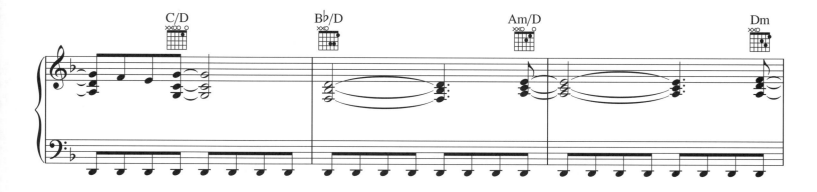

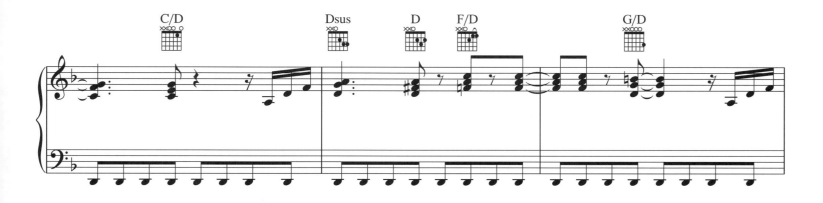

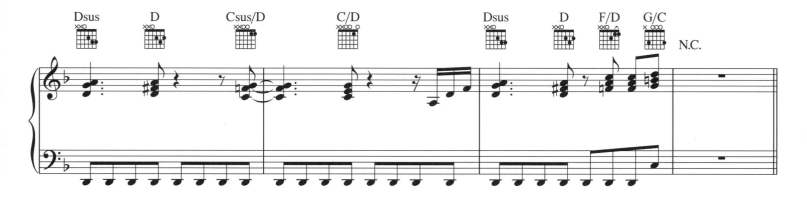

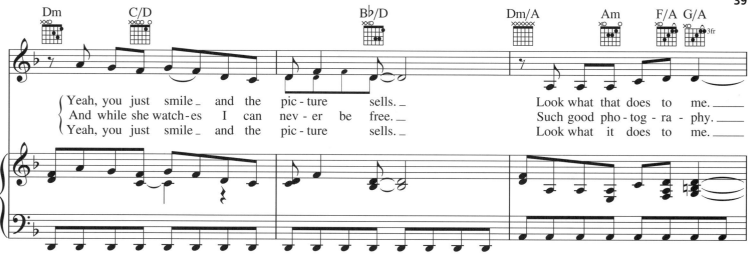

Yeah, you just smile_ and the pic - ture sells. _ Look what that does to me. _____
And while she watch - es I can nev - er be free. _ Such good pho - tog - ra - phy. _____
Yeah, you just smile_ and the pic - ture sells. _ Look what it does to me. _____

I'll wait _ till your love comes down. _

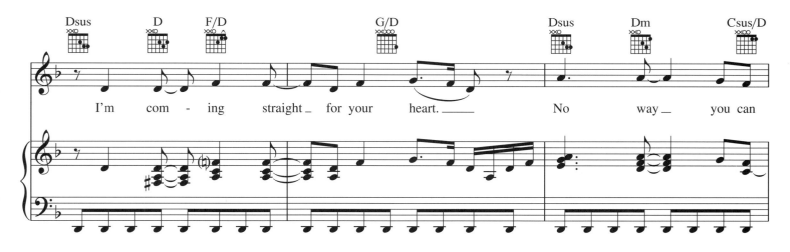

I'm com - ing straight _ for your heart. _____ No way _ you can

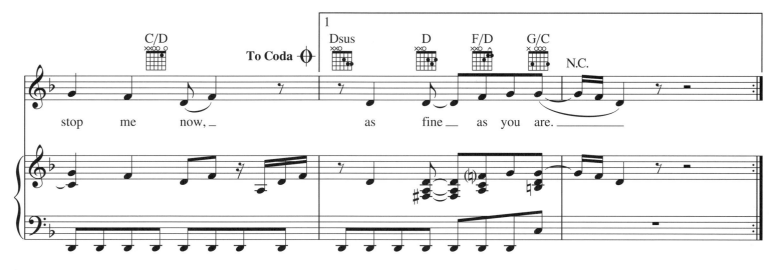

stop me now, _ as fine _ as you are. _____

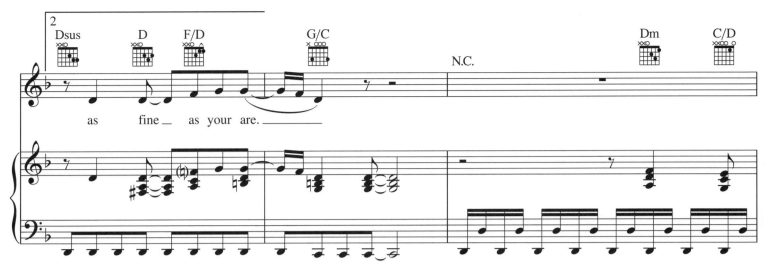

as fine __ as your are. _____

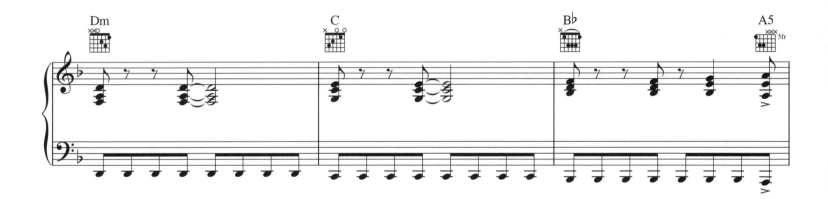

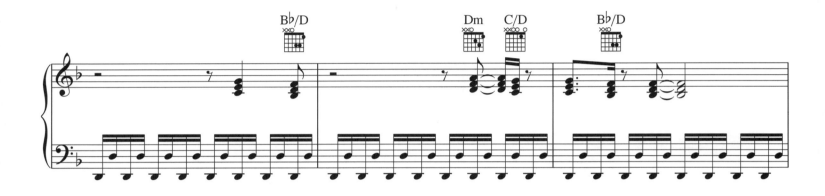

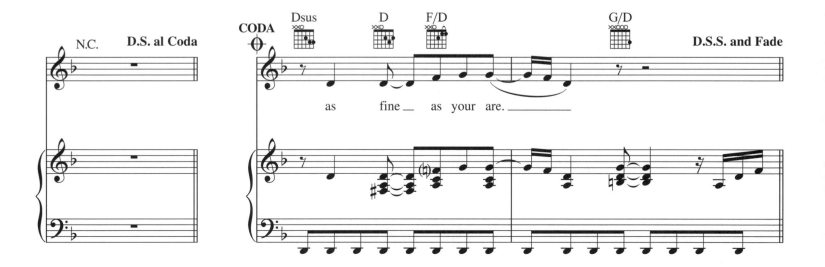

as fine __ as your are. _____

JUMP

Words and Music by DAVID LEE ROTH,
EDWARD VAN HALEN, ALEX VAN HALEN
and MICHAEL ANTHONY

Bright Rock

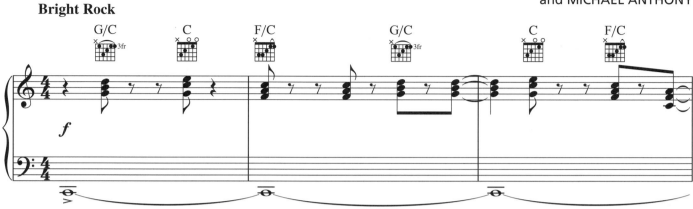

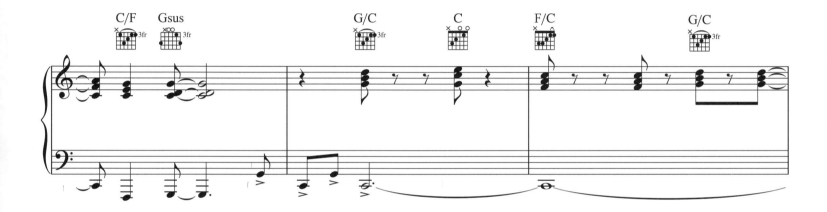

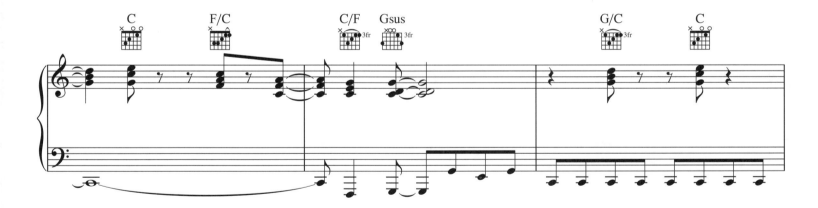

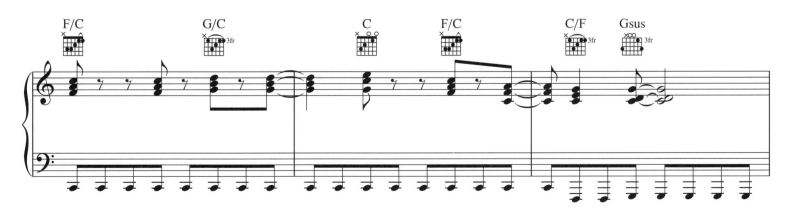

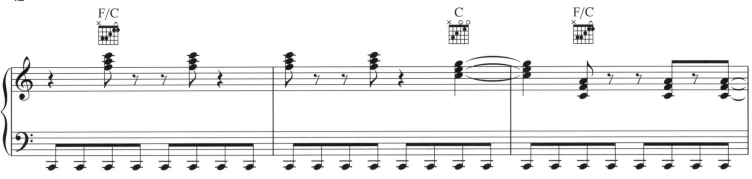

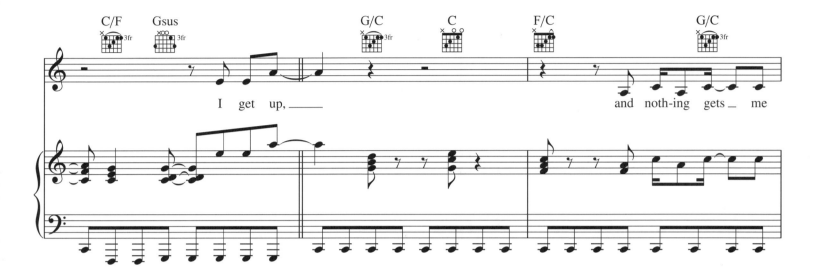

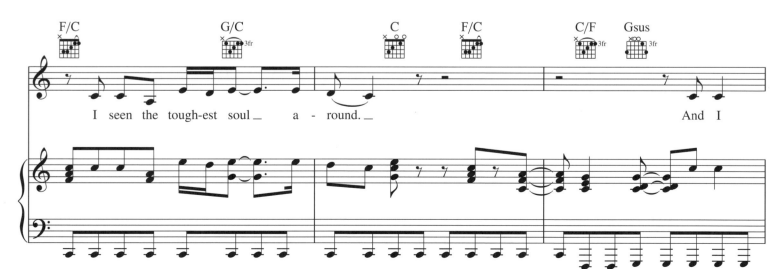

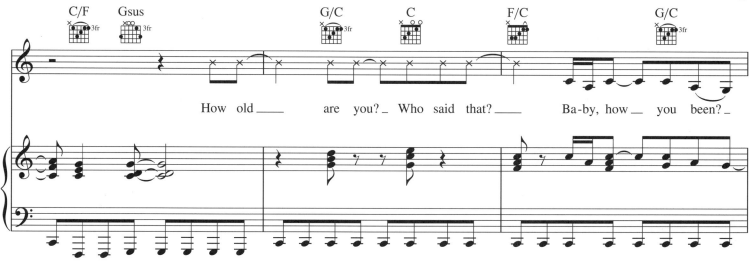

How old ___ are you? ___ Who said that? ___ Ba-by, how ___ you been? ___

You say you don't know. _____ You won't

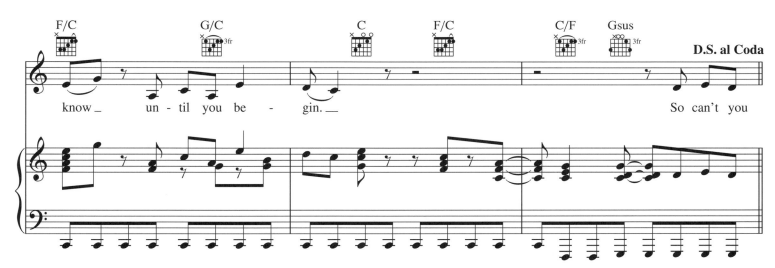

D.S. al Coda

know ___ un - til you be - gin. ___ So can't you

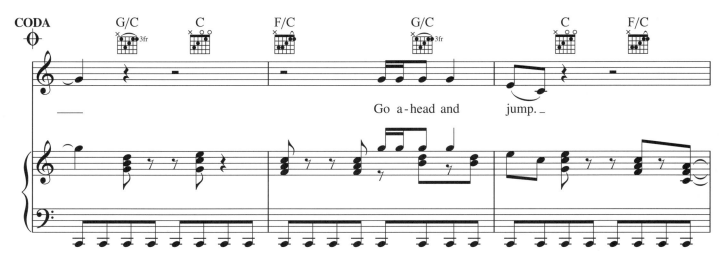

CODA

___ Go a-head and jump. ___

Jump!

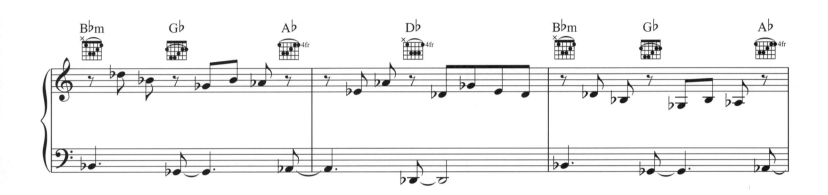

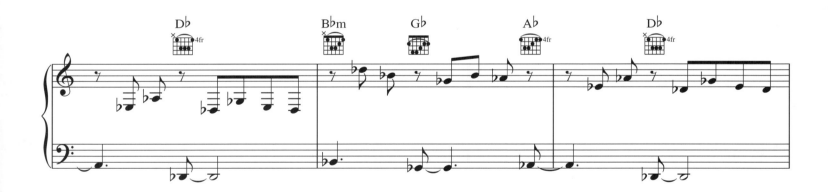

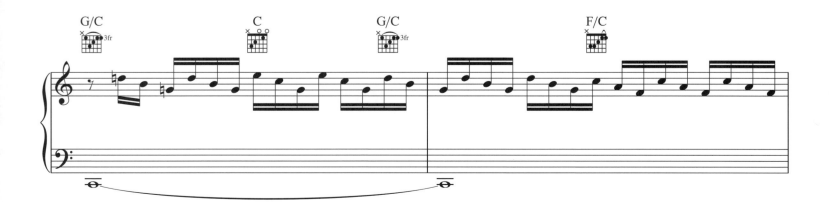

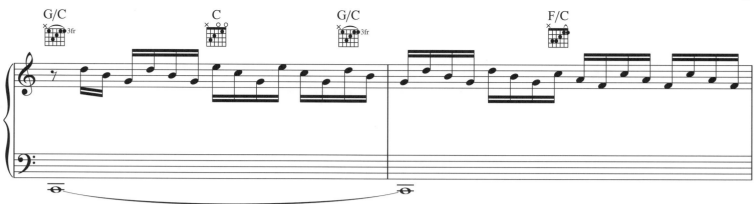

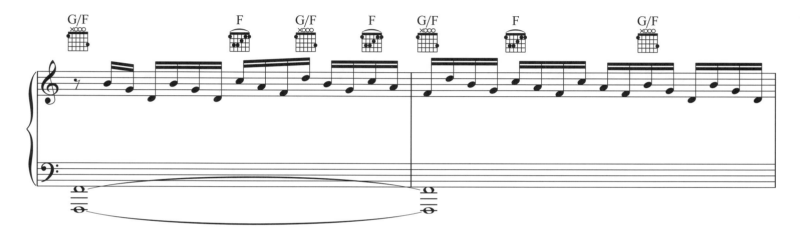

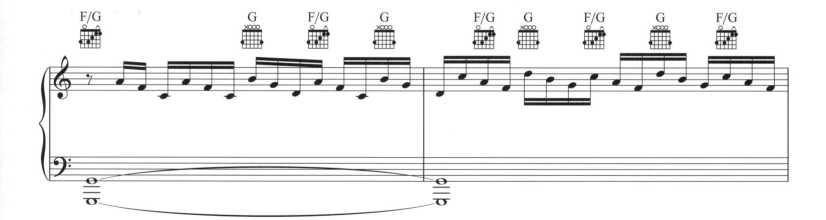

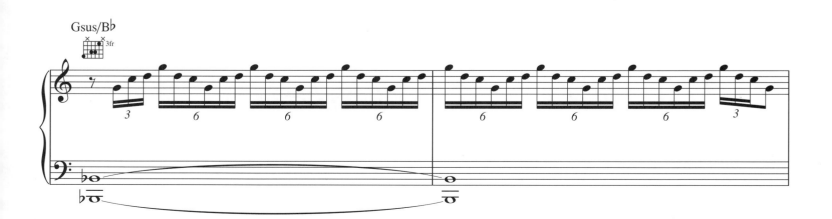

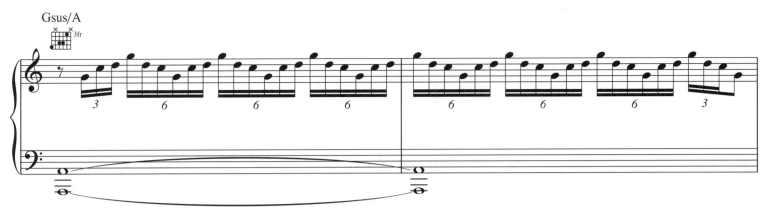

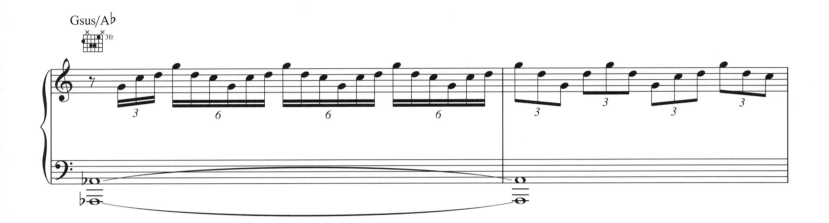

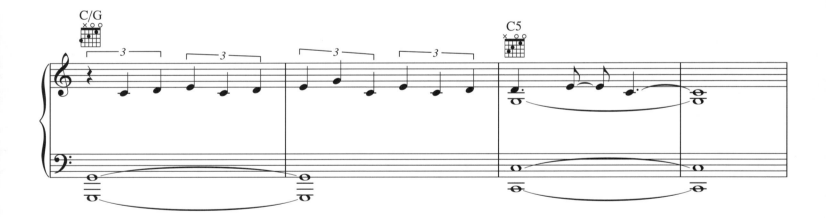

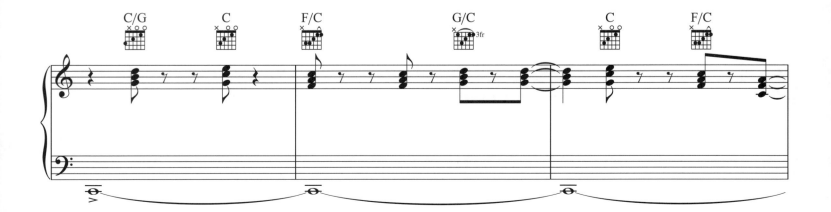

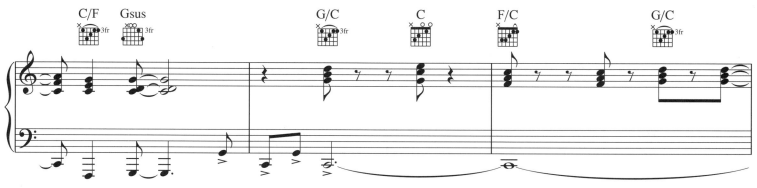

Might as well jump.

Vocal ad lib.

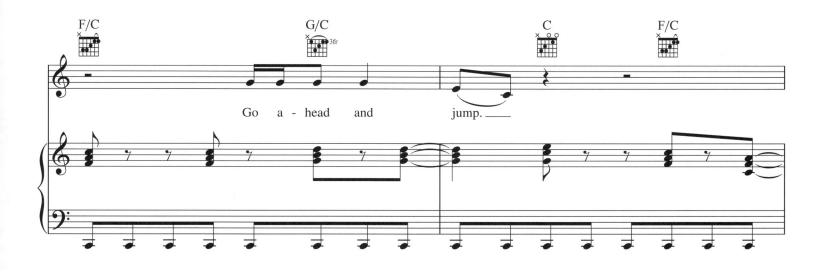

Go a - head and jump. ____

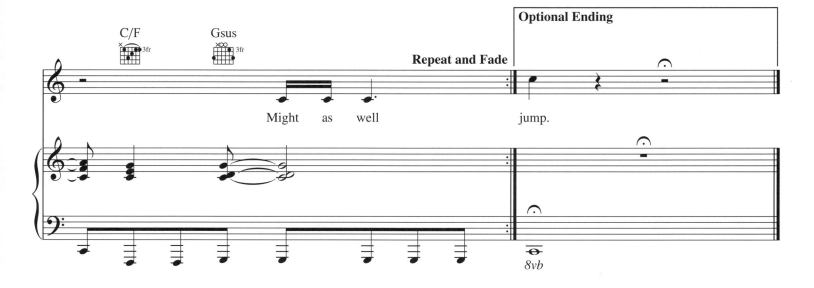

Optional Ending

Repeat and Fade

Might as well jump.

8vb

JUST A GIGOLO/I AIN'T GOT NOBODY
(And Nobody Cares for Me)

Just a Gigolo
Original German Text by JULIUS BRAMMER
English Words by IRVING CAESAR
Music by LEONELLO CASUCCI

I Ain't Got Nobody
Words BY ROGER GRAHAM
Music by SPENCER WILLIAMS and DAVE PEYTON

JUST LIKE PARADISE

Words by DAVID LEE ROTH
Music by BRETT TUGGLE

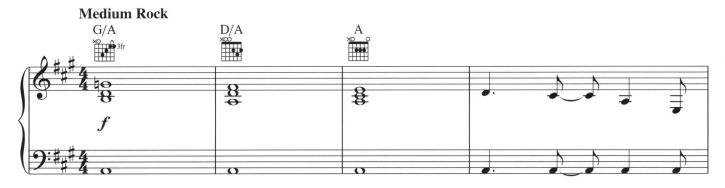

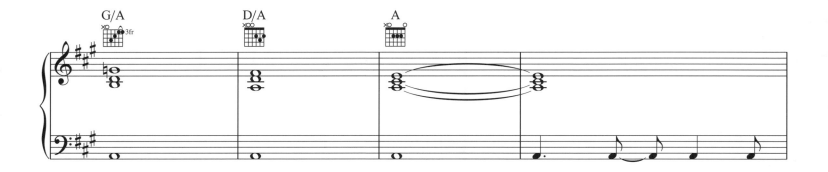

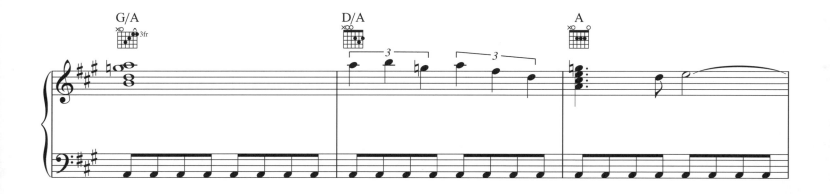

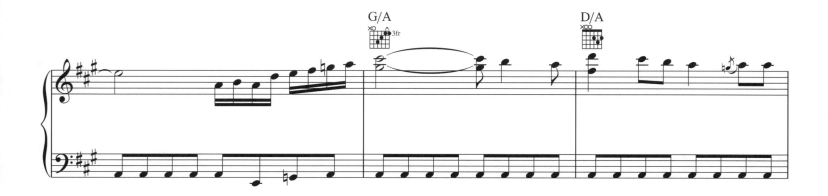

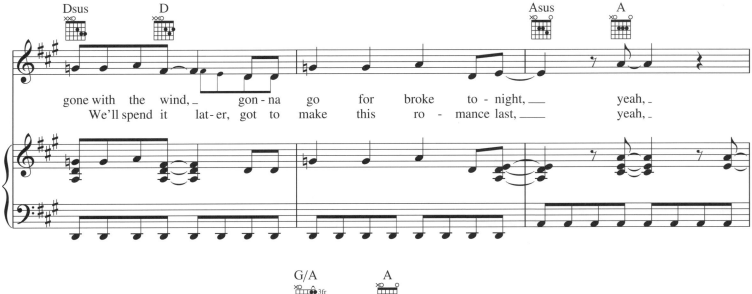

gone with the wind, _ gon-na go for broke to-night, ___ yeah, _
We'll spend it lat-er, got to make this ro - mance last, ___ yeah, _

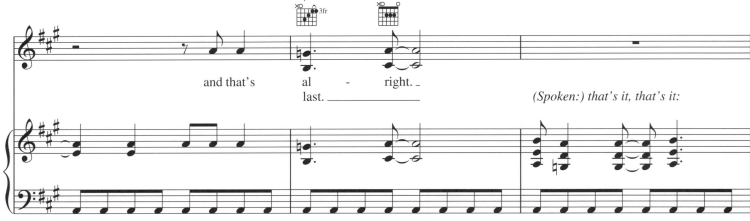

and that's al - right. _
last. _____

(Spoken:) that's it, that's it:

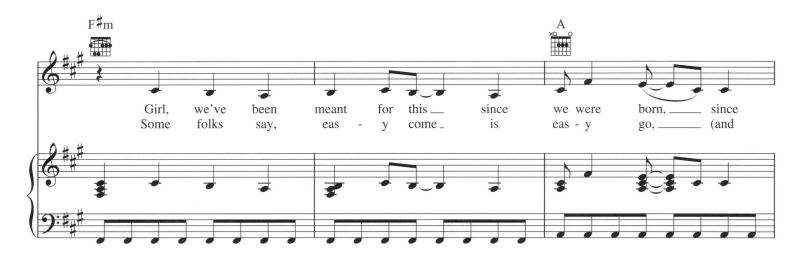

Girl, we've been meant for this __ since we were born, ___ since
Some folks say, eas - y come _ is eas - y go, _____ (and

we were born. ___ No prob-lems now, _ (the coast __ is clear,) _ it's
some folks say,) ___ but one night ain't _ e - nough _ for me, ___ girl,

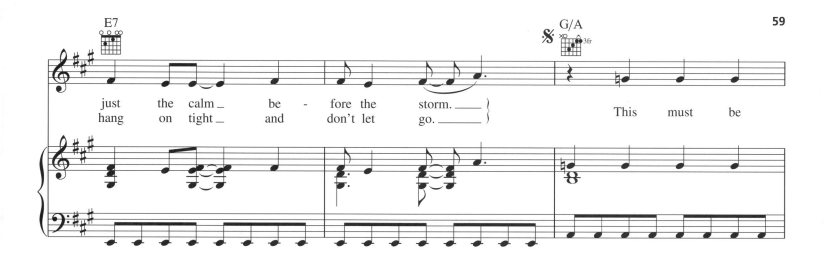

just the calm___ be - fore the storm.___ This must be
hang on tight___ and don't let go.___

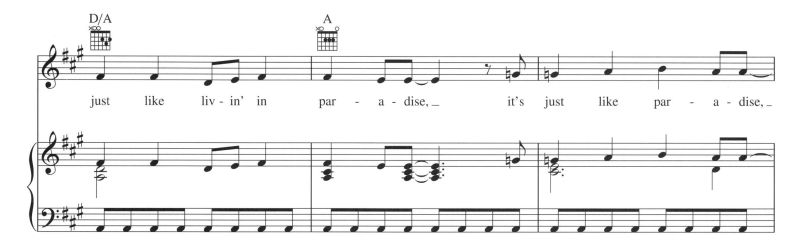

just like liv-in' in par - a - dise,___ it's just like par - a - dise,___

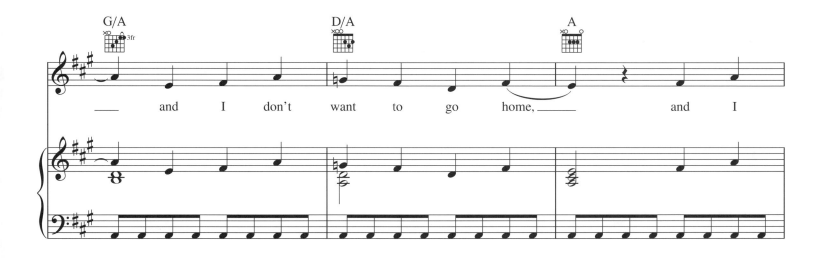

___ and I don't want to go home,_____ and I

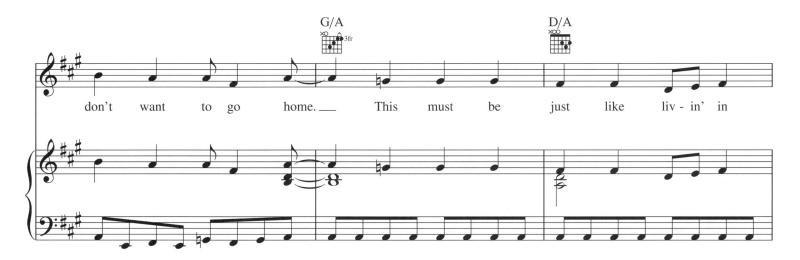

don't want to go home.___ This must be just like liv-in' in

par - a - dise, ____ and I don't

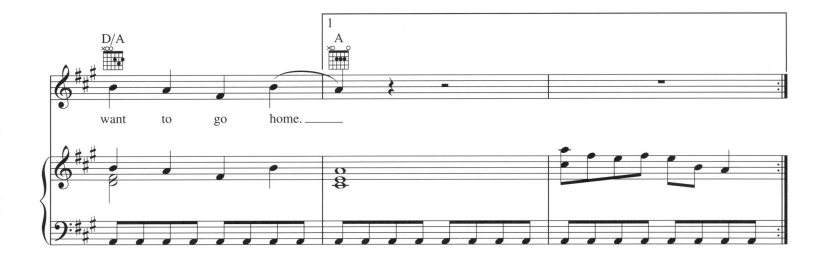

want to go home. ____

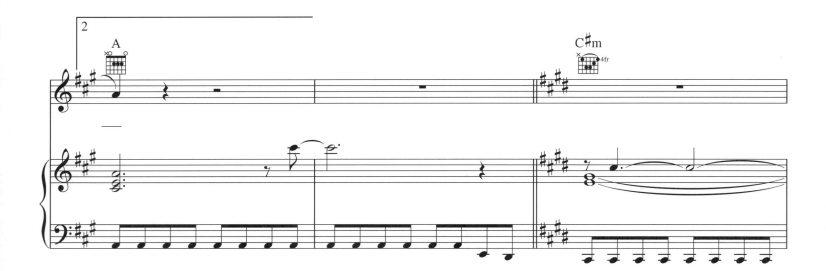

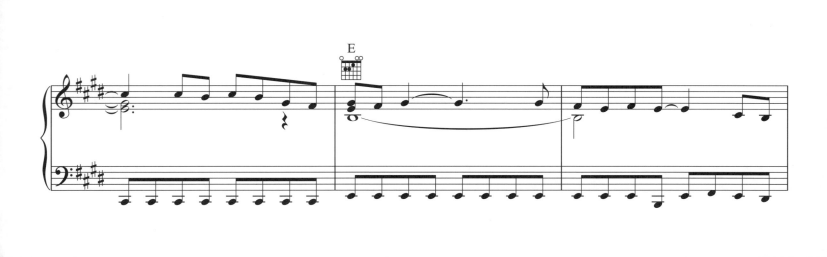

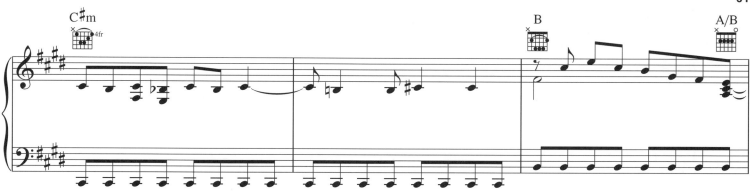

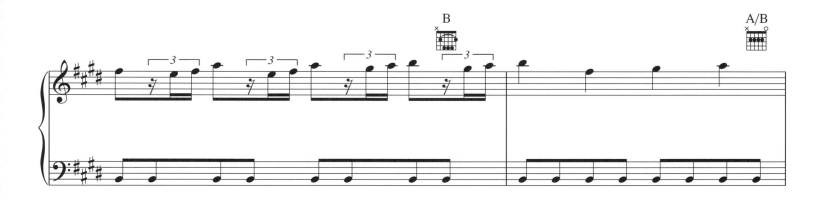

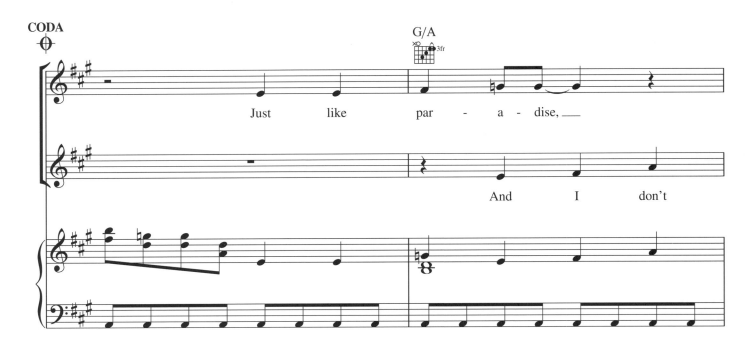

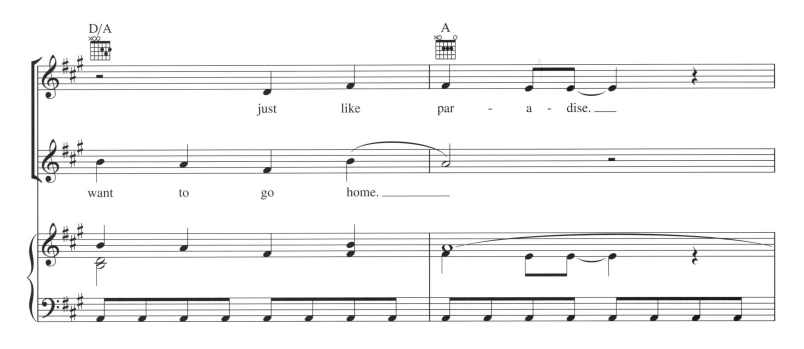

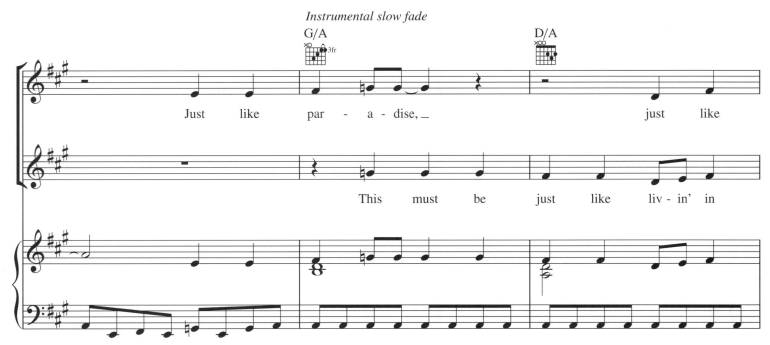

OH, PRETTY WOMAN

Words and Music by ROY ORBISON
and BILL DEES

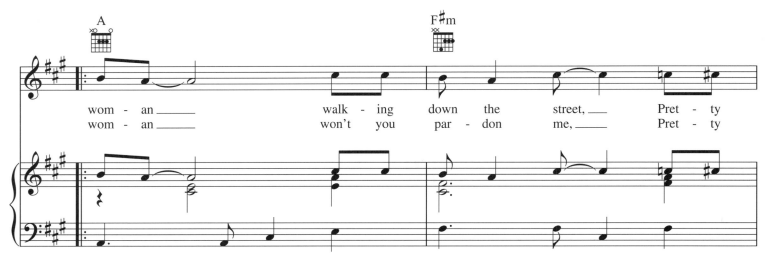

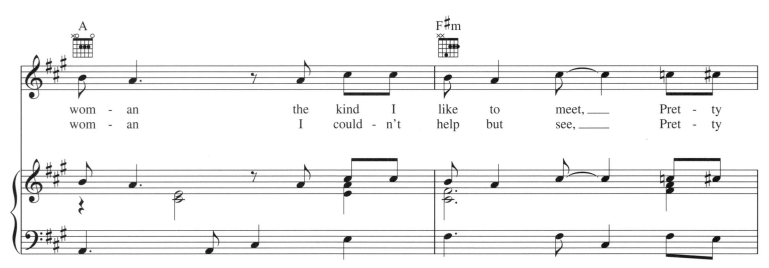

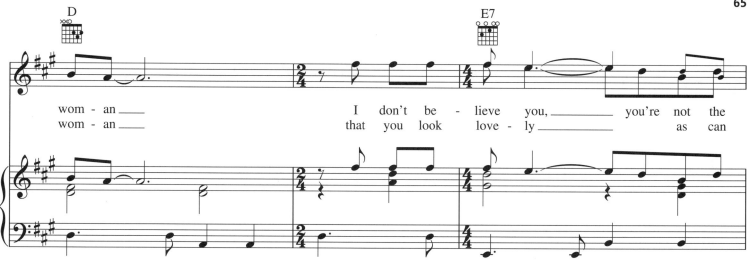

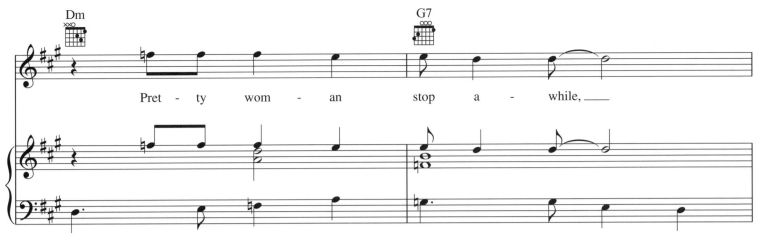

Pret - ty wom - an stop a - while, ___

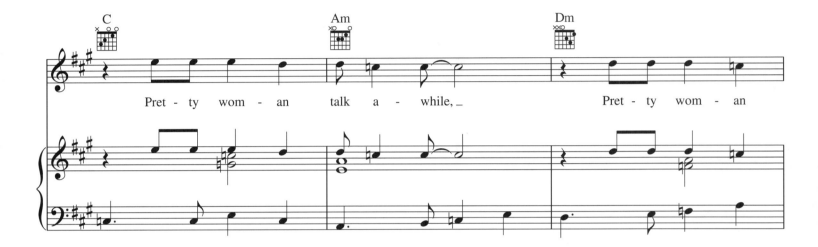

Pret - ty wom - an talk a - while, _ Pret - ty wom - an

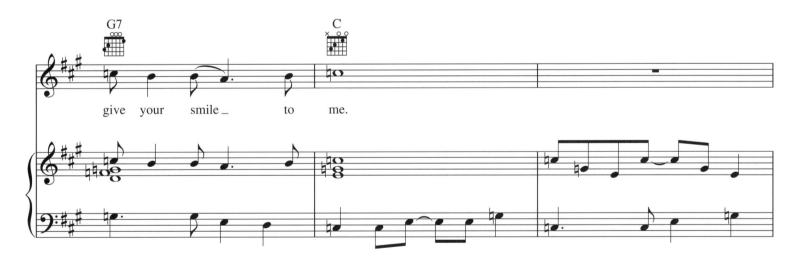

give your smile _ to me.

Pret - ty wom - an yeah, yeah, yeah, _____ Pret - ty wom - an

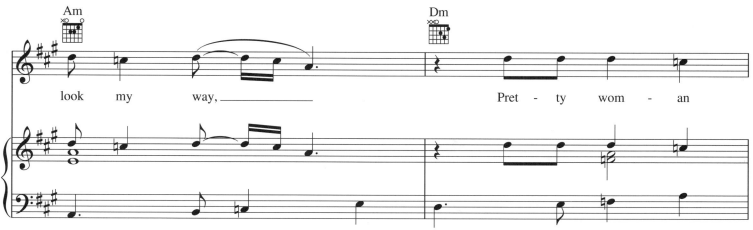

look my way, _____ Pret - ty wom - an

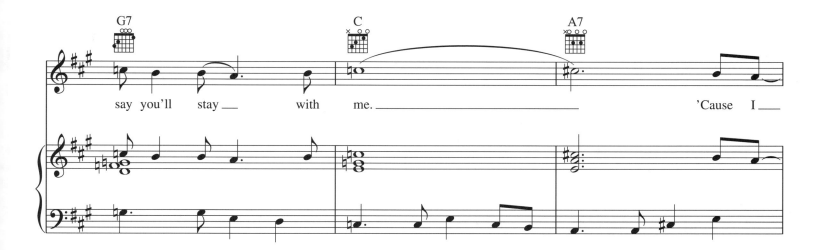

say you'll stay ___ with me. _____ 'Cause I ___

___ need you ___ I'll treat you right.

Come with me ba - by. ___ Be mine to -

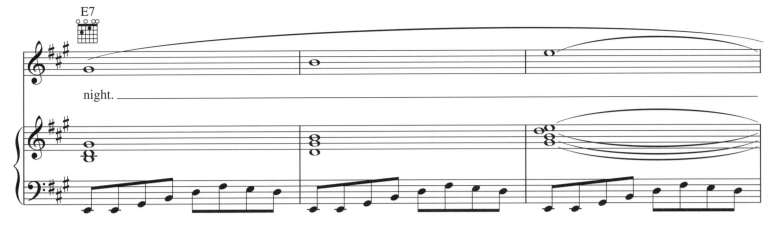

night. _____

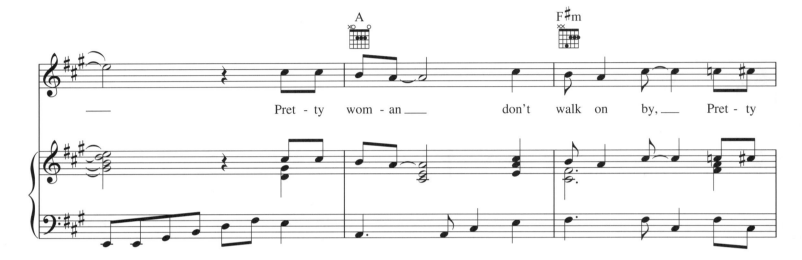

Pret - ty wom - an ____ don't walk on by, ____ Pret - ty

wom - an ____ don't make me cry, ____ Pret - ty

wom - an ____ don't walk a - way. ____

Hey, O. K.

If that's the way it must be ___ O. K.

I guess I'll go on home, ___ it's late ___ There'll be to-

mor - row night but wait! What do I see? ___

UNCHAINED

Words and Music by DAVID LEE ROTH,
EDWARD VAN HALEN, ALEX VAN HALEN
and MICHAEL ANTHONY

Medium Rock beat

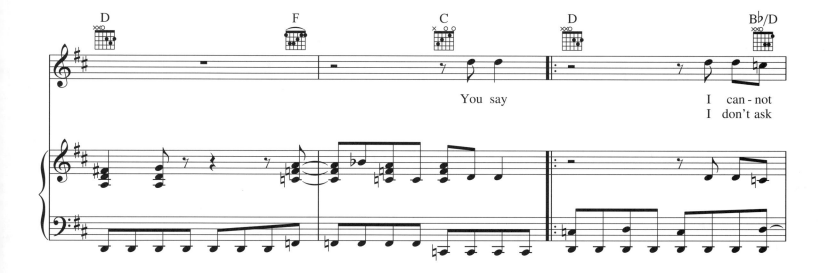

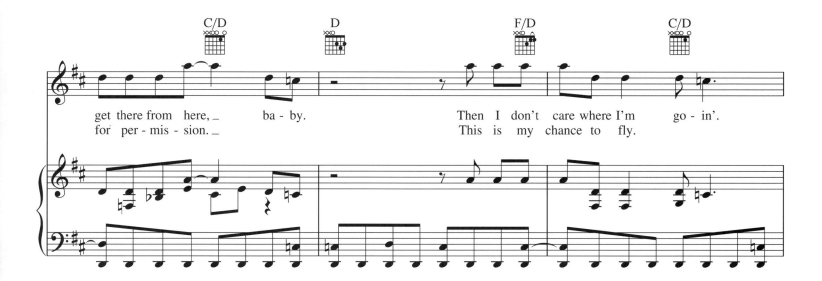

And you hit ___ the ground run - nin'. Change. _ Ain't noth - in'

stays the same. Un - chained. _ Yeah, you hit ___ the ground run - nin'. Change. _

PANAMA

Words and Music by DAVID LEE ROTH,
EDWARD VAN HALEN and ALEX VAN HALEN

Bright Rock beat

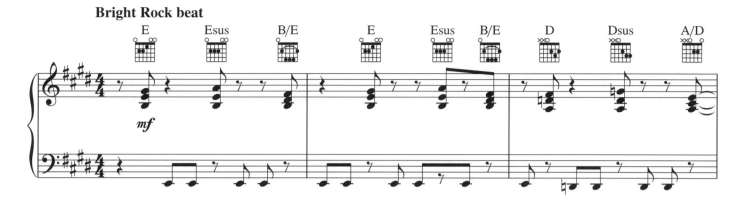

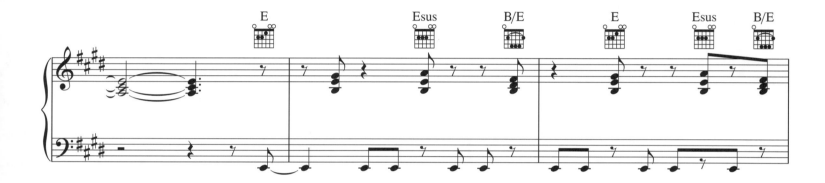

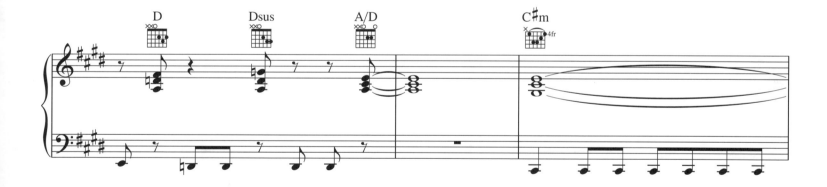

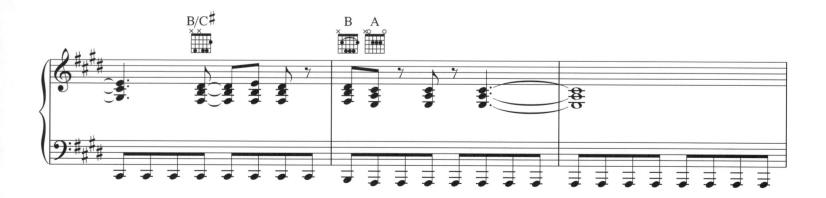

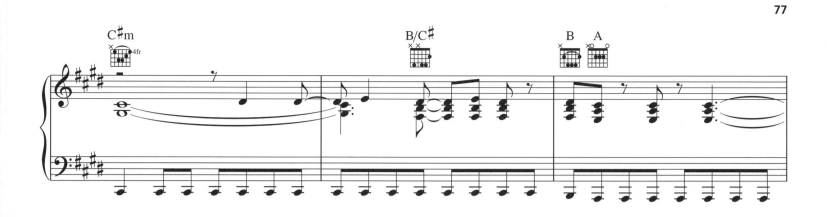

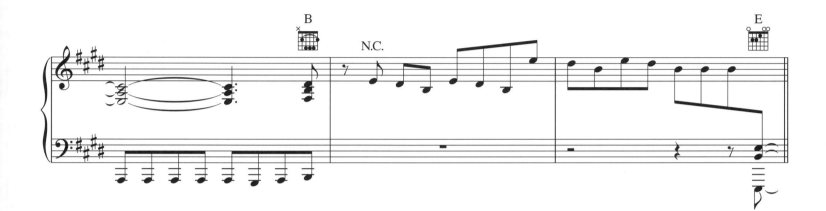

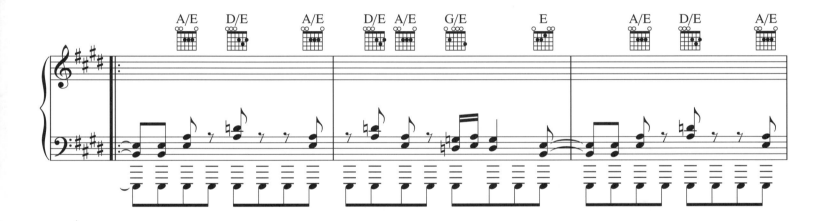

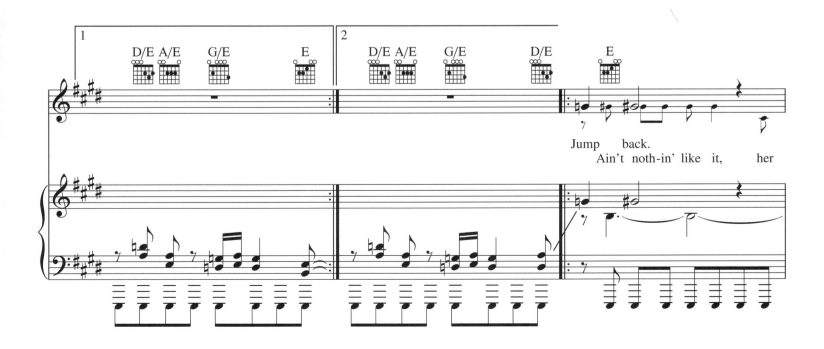

Jump   back.

Ain't noth-in' like it,   her

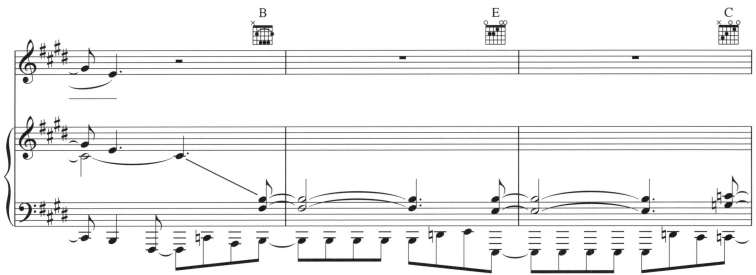

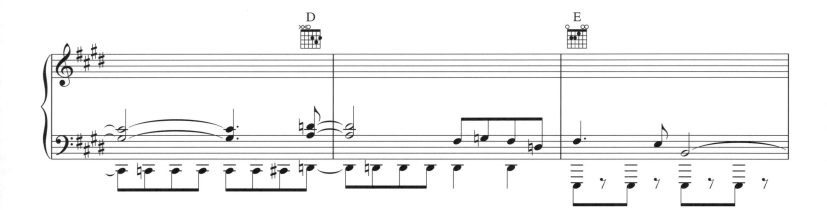

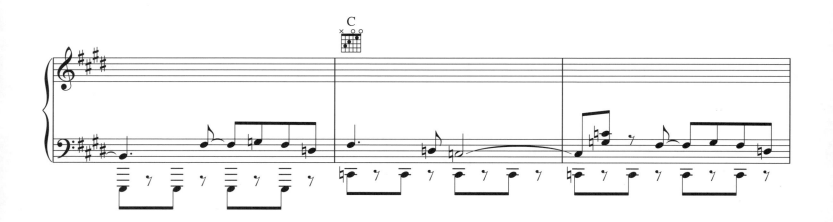

THAT'S LIFE

Words and Music by DEAN KAY
and KELLY GORDON

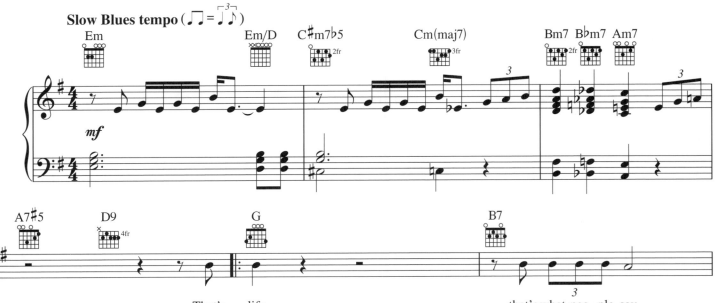

That's life, that's what peo-ple say.

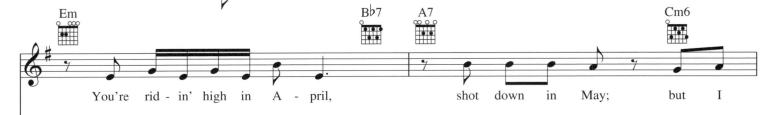

You're rid-in' high in A-pril, shot down in May; but I

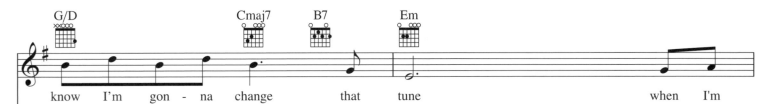

know I'm gon-na change that tune when I'm

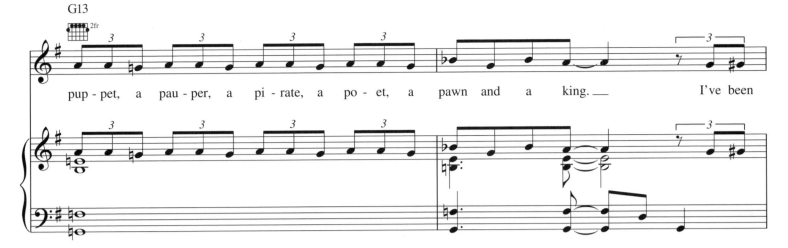

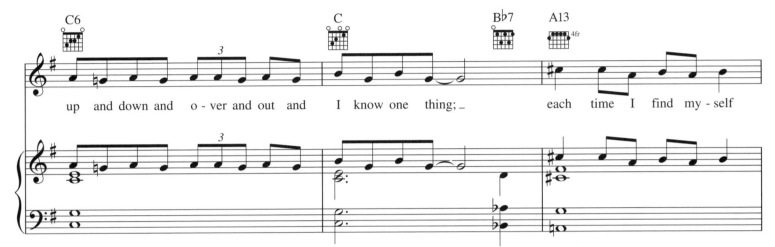

pup-pet, a pau-per, a pi-rate, a po-et, a pawn and a king. ___ I've been

up and down and o-ver and out and I know one thing; ___ each time I find my-self

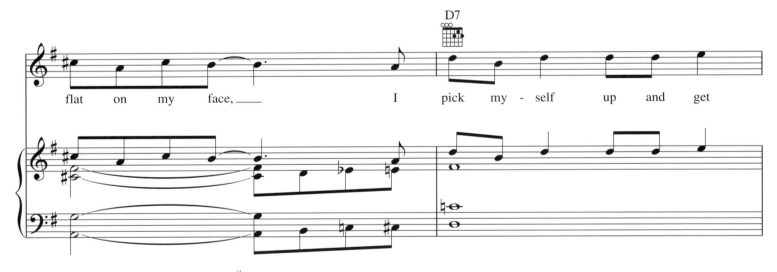

flat on my face, ___ I pick my-self up and get

back in the race. ___ That's life, I can't de-ny it.

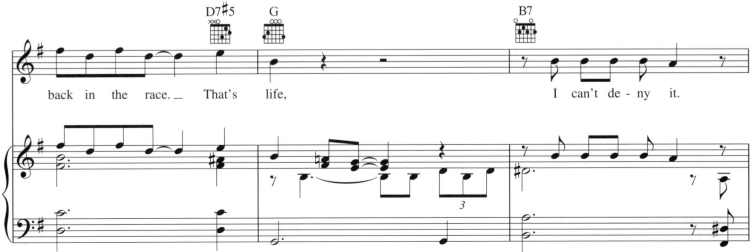

YANKEE ROSE

Words by DAVID LEE ROTH
Music by STEVE VAI

Are you read-y for the new sen-sa-tion? Well, here's the shot heard
walks, watch, the sparks will fly, fire-crack-in' on the

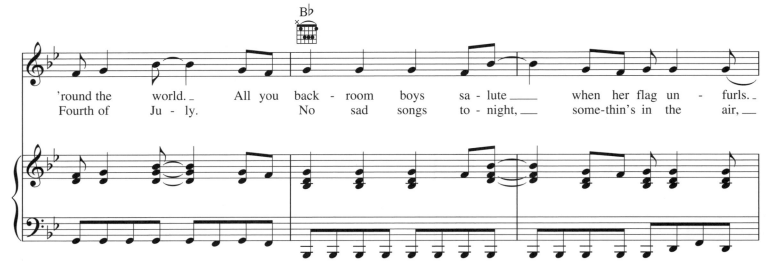

'round the world. All you back-room boys sa-lute when her flag un-furls.
Fourth of Ju-ly. No sad songs to-night, some-thin's in the air,

Well, guess who's back in
she's a real state of

cir - cu - la - tion? Now, I don't know what you may have heard, _ but what I
in - de - pen - dents. So pret - ty when her rock - ets glare. _

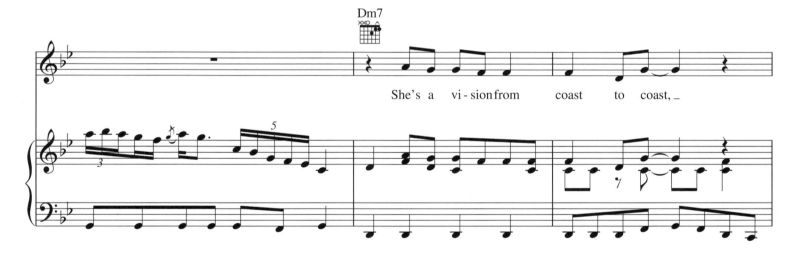

B♭

G5

need right now's the o - rig - i - nal good time girl. ___ }
Still prov - in' an - y night that her flag's still there. ___ }

Dm7

She's a vi - sion from coast to coast, _

F/B♭

Dm7

sea to shin - ing sea. _____ Hey, sis - ter, you're the

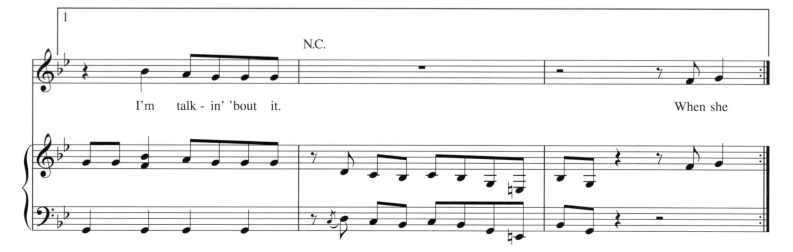

I'm in love with the Yan-kee Rose. Ah!

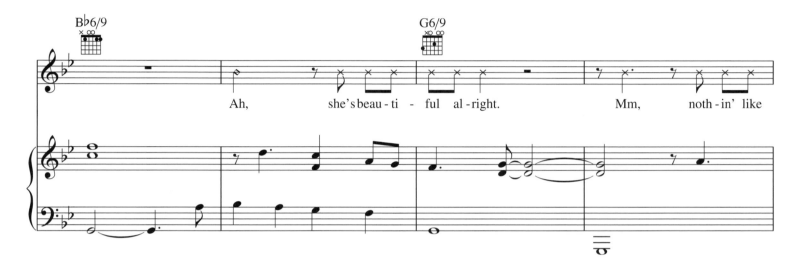

Ah, she's beau-ti-ful al-right. Mm, noth-in' like

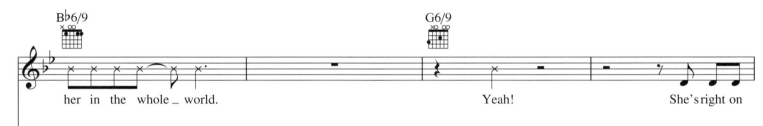

her in the whole world. Yeah! She's right on

time. I'm on the case. Pick up the phone, no time to

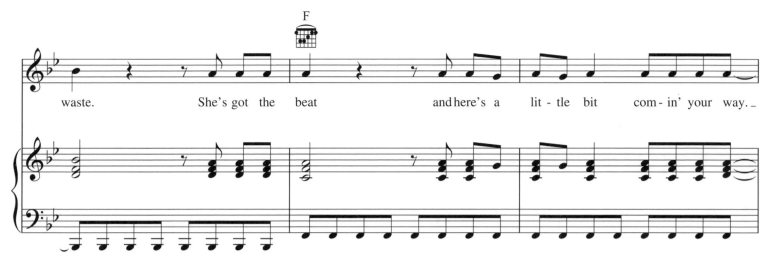

waste. She's got the beat and here's a lit - tle bit com - in' your way. __

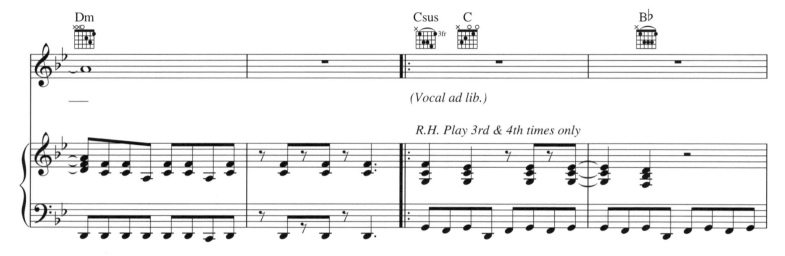

(Vocal ad lib.)

R.H. Play 3rd & 4th times only

Bright lights,

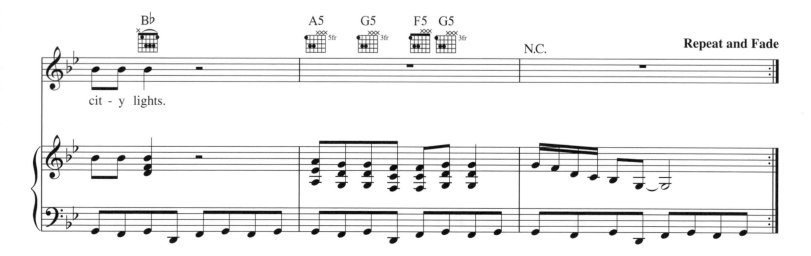

cit - y lights.